SIGHT READING SUCCESS
PIANO GRADE 2
MALCOLM RILEY & PAUL TERRY

RHINEGOLD EDUCATION

WWW.RHINEGOLDEDUCATION.CO.UK

FOR STUDENTS

Sight reading is an important and enjoyable musical skill. The more you practise the better you will get, and working carefully through this book will help you.

Use the CD included with this book to hear how the pieces should sound. Listen to the music carefully to check your playing. Most of the written instructions are also spoken for you on the CD. The tracks can be downloaded onto an MP3 player if you find that easier to use next to the piano.

From the beginning of the book to piece 36 you should listen to the recording of each piece first to hear how it should sound (except when you are asked to do otherwise). Then play the music on the piano, copying what you have heard. From piece 38 onwards, make sure that you play first and then afterwards listen to check your playing was correct. Up to piece 64 there are spoken hints to help you, but after that you are on your own!

Tick the box when you have finished each section or piece, so that you know which ones you have tried – it's not sight reading if you keep playing the same pieces!

If you find any of the examples on the CD are too fast when you are starting out, there are software programs available on the internet that can slow down the speed of music on any CD played on a computer. One that is free to download is: **Speedshifter** (available from www.abrsm.org/en/students/speedshifter).

FOR TEACHERS

This book follows the sight reading requirements for the Grade 2 piano exam of the Associated Board of the Royal Schools of Music (as revised in 2009). It is also suitable for all piano students who wish to improve their sight reading skills.

A unique feature of the books in this series is the inclusion of a specially-recorded CD which students can use at home for additional guidance, and to check the accuracy of their own playing. Encourage your students to use it as a tool to evaluate their own playing and learn from their mistakes, as well as a support for when you are not there to help.

Sight Reading Success progressively introduces each of the elements in sight reading, along with many useful tips and exercises to improve fluency. Each book builds on the skills taught in the previous volumes, so it is recommended that your students work through Grade 1 before starting on this book.

The second part of the book includes exam-standard pieces to play in lessons or at home. Take a few minutes in every lesson to check progress and help with any difficulties, and encourage regular sight reading so that students have confidence when going into their exam.

Tick boxes are provided for students to record their progress through the book.

USING A METRONOME

A **metronome** is a device that will click a regular pulse at any speed you wish to help you keep in time when practising. There are several on the internet and the one at www.metronomeonline.com is free and easy to use. The numbers around the dial indicate the speed in beats (or pulses) per minute: the higher the number, the faster the speed.

RHYTHM AND TEMPO

 1 Grade 2 sight reading uses the same time signatures as Grade 1 – ⅔, ¾ and 4/4 – but there are some extra note lengths to learn.

A **semibreve** (or whole note) (𝐨) lasts for four beats.

Listen to track 2 and count along with the pulse, watching out for the semibreves.

 2

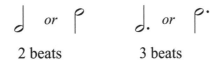

Now play this on the piano. Remember to count as evenly as you can, and hold the last note down for four full beats.

DOTTED NOTES

 3 A dot *after* a note increases its length by half. For example, a minim (or half note) is two beats long, so a dotted minim (or dotted half note) will be three beats long:

Be careful not to confuse this type of dot with a dot *above* or *below* a note which means *staccato*.

4 In this piece count along with the pulse, watching out for the dotted minim.

Now play this on the piano. Count yourself in before starting.

5 Dotted minims are often used in ¾ time. Listen to track 6 and get ready to play it with your left hand. Don't forget to hold the last note for three full beats.

6

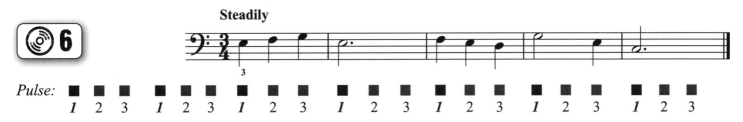

☐ **TICK THE BOX WHEN YOU HAVE COMPLETED THIS PAGE**

7 You will also see **dotted crotchets** (or dotted quarter notes) in Grade 2 sight reading. A crotchet is worth one beat and the dot increases this by half, so a dotted crotchet is worth one and a half beats. In Grade 2 a dotted crotchet is always followed by a single quaver (or eighth note) to make a two-beat pattern (𝅘𝅥. 𝅘𝅥𝅮).

When counting this pattern, slip 'and' between the beats to position the quaver correctly:

Notice that there are *two* counts during a dotted crotchet, although you must then play the quaver before the next count begins, as you can see above.

 8 Listen to hear how to count the dotted crotchets in the next tune.

Now play this on the piano. Remember to count the pulse as you play.

 9 In the next tune the dotted crotchets come on different beats of the bar, so listen carefully to the recording before you play it. If you find it tricky, listen again and then have another go.

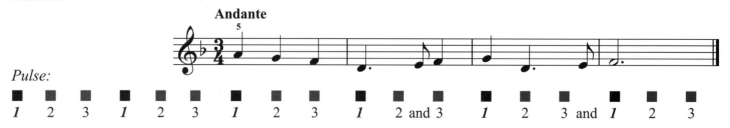

TICK THE BOX WHEN YOU HAVE COMPLETED THIS SECTION ☐

TIED NOTES

 10 A **tie** is a curved line which joins two notes next to each other that have the *same* pitch. Tied notes become a single sound so, in the next example, you would only play one note but make it last for four beats.

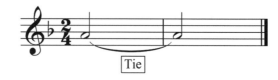

It is easy to confuse a tie with a **slur**. A slur is a curved line above or below notes of *different* pitches that means they should be played smoothly. Sometimes a slur can include a tied note, as shown in the second example:

If a note with an accidental is tied, the accidental is not printed again on the second note because the tie means you carry on holding down the first note. But if the same black note is needed later in the bar, there will be an accidental before the note, as shown here in bar 2:

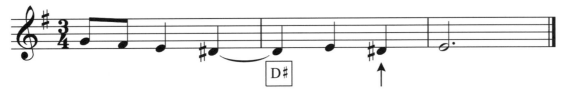

Ties are used to extend the length of a note across a barline, as in the example above. They are also used to create notes of unusual lengths, as in piece 12 where the long note in the second bar lasts for two and a half beats.

 Listen to the recording of this tune to hear how to count the tied note. Play the piece on the piano after listening.

 In this tune, the first pair of tied notes lasts for three beats, and the second pair lasts for five beats. Listen carefully to how these long notes are counted and then play the tune on the piano. Don't forget that the key signature tells you to play F♯s in the first and last bars.

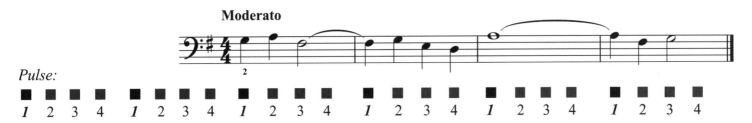

TEMPO

 Most words for describing the tempo (or speed) of a piece in Grade 2 sight reading are the same as those you learned for Grade 1, but you should also learn the following new terms:

- A **waltz** is a ballroom dance in $\frac{3}{4}$ time. It is usually played at a medium to fairly fast speed.

- A **minuet** is an older style of dance in $\frac{3}{4}$ time, and is usually a little slower than a waltz. The Italian phrase *Tempo di minuetto* means 'At the speed of a minuet'.

- **Espressivo** is an Italian word meaning 'expressively'. You may see it used with one of the Italian words for tempo that you already know. For example, *Andante espressivo* means 'fairly slow and expressively'.

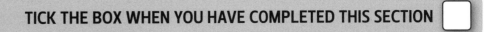 **TICK THE BOX WHEN YOU HAVE COMPLETED THIS SECTION**

HANDS TOGETHER

 The most important new feature in Grade 2 sight reading is playing with both hands together. To do this your eyes have to read both staves at the same time. This is only really possible if you can avoid looking at your fingers as you play.

Practise closing your eyes and gently gliding your fingers over the keys to feel the groups of two and three black notes. From these you can find all the notes just by touch. For example, C is just to the left of a group of two black notes.

Try playing some scales and broken chords with your eyes shut, or play in the dark! Once you can find the notes without looking at the keys you know you can keep your eyes on the music when you are sight reading. This is something that might take quite a bit of practice, but it will make a big difference to your sight reading.

LOOK AHEAD

 When sight reading, look ahead to what happens next. Watch for patterns – are the notes going up or down, or are they staying at the same pitch? For example, piece 17 starts with repeated notes in one hand and then the other, and then the right hand comes down a scale.

At first you may find it difficult to look more than one beat ahead of where you are playing, but the more you practise sight reading the more you will notice about the music coming up.

Practise with these simple exercises. The most important thing is to keep an even pulse – don't hesitate in order to look at your fingers. Compare your playing with the recording after you have finished each piece. It doesn't matter if you play more slowly than the recording, just keep to a regular pulse.

Remember to get both your hands into position before you start each exercise, using the given fingering as a guide. Count yourself in with two bars of beats. There are reminders about black notes for you.

 This exercise is not too difficult if you notice that both hands play G all through the first two bars, then the right hand plays a scale passage, and the left hand only plays C and G in the last bar.

 The only left-hand notes in this piece are C, B and G, so concentrate on the right-hand part.

19 Look out for the left-hand pattern in this piece. It goes up the first five notes of a scale and back down again. You then just have to think about the last two notes in this part.

20 Look out for the key signature, and get your finger ready to play the F♯ before you start.

21 Every note in this piece is one step away from its neighbours, except for the last two notes in the left hand, so you shouldn't need to stop to search for notes. Don't forget to check the key signature before starting to play.

22 Each pair of tied semibreves should last for eight beats. These long notes let you concentrate on the music in the other hand during the first four bars.

The G♯ accidentals, and the fact that the piece begins and ends on an A, tell you that the key is A minor. Don't forget that there are two G♯s in the third bar, because the accidental also changes any notes of the same pitch that come later in the same bar.

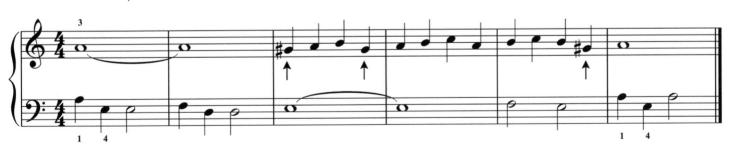

23 Look for the falling-scale pattern in the left hand at the start of this piece, which will allow you to focus on the busier right-hand part.

The key signature and accidentals tell you that the key is D minor, and you will notice that the music begins and ends on a D. The B♭ in the key signature is cancelled by a B♮ in bar 3: in minor keys the sixth note of the scale is sometimes altered by an accidental like this.

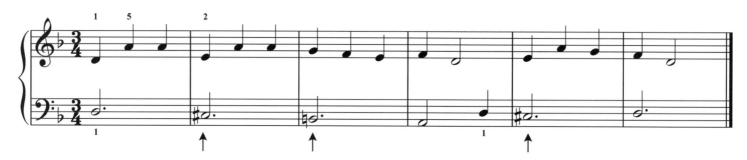

TICK THE BOX WHEN YOU HAVE COMPLETED THIS SECTION ☐

THREE NEW KEYS

 24 The previous exercises were in the five keys that you learned for Grade 1 sight reading:

- C major (no key signature)

- F major (key signature of B♭)

- G major (key signature of F♯)

- A minor (no key signature, plus G♯ accidental)

- D minor (key signature of B♭, plus C♯ accidental)

Grade 2 sight reading can be in any of these keys, *or* in one of three new keys (E minor, D major or G minor) that you may already know from playing scales.

E MINOR

 25 E minor has the same key signature as G major. This is F# and it tells you that every F in the music is to be played as an F#.

E minor also has an accidental for D# and sometimes for C# as well. Remember that accidentals also affect notes of the *same* pitch that come later in the *same* bar.

Before you start a piece of sight reading, look out for any black notes required and hover the fingers of both hands over the notes you will need to play. Use the fingering given as a guide.

In the next piece the black notes are marked with arrows, but in the pieces after that you must find them for yourself. After trying each piece, compare your playing with the recording.

 26 Quiet *legato* playing will help to create a gentle mood for this piece.

Smooth and gentle

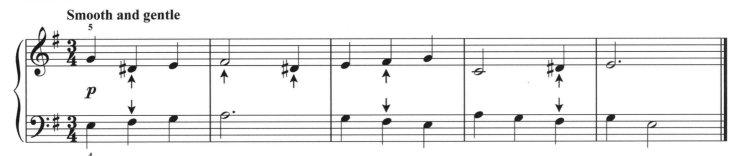

 27 Try to bring out the contrast between the staccato quavers and sustained longer notes. Make sure you hold the final tied notes for their full three beats.

Brightly

 28 Before you start to play, find all the black notes you will need for this piece, looking at the key signature and the accidentals. It should be played slowly and sadly.

A sad song

TICK THE BOX WHEN YOU HAVE COMPLETED THIS SECTION ☐

D MAJOR

 D major has a key signature of two sharps, F♯ and C♯.

In the next piece the black notes are marked with arrows, but in the pieces after that you must find them for yourself. Afterwards compare your playing with the recording.

 Make a clear change from loud to soft halfway through this piece. Don't worry if you need to play it more slowly than the recording, but remember that a march should have a firm rhythm to keep the soldiers' feet in time.

 Remember that a minuet is a dance, so play this piece with a spring in the rhythm.

 Use the staccato notes and accents to create a playful mood, and keep to a firm pulse in the last two bars.

TICK THE BOX WHEN YOU HAVE COMPLETED THIS SECTION ☐

G MINOR

 G minor has a key signature of two flats, Bb and Eb, and an accidental for F♯. Sometimes there is also an accidental for E♮, which temporarily cancels the Eb in the key signature for that note and any others of the *same* pitch that come later in the *same* bar.

In the next piece the black notes are marked with arrows, but in the pieces after that you must find them for yourself. Afterwards compare your playing with the recording.

 When you place your hands in position at the start, make sure your fingers hover over any black notes needed. There are several to think about in this piece, but the arrows will help you find them.

The music is soft (*p*) at the beginning, and at the end it should fade away to **pp**, which means *very soft*.

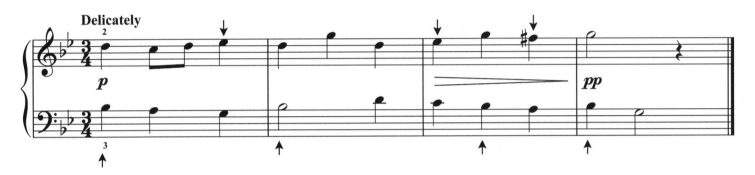

In this piece aim for a clear contrast between the loud, accented notes in bar 3, and the quiet, delicate ending.

Check the key signature and accidentals before you starting playing this piece. The slurs show you that you need to play smoothly.

TICK THE BOX WHEN YOU HAVE COMPLETED THIS SECTION	☐

ON YOUR OWN

 Now you need plenty of practice in playing new pieces! The more you can do, the easier sight reading will become.

Work through the rest of this book, and use the recordings to check your playing. If you hear differences, try to work out why. Tick the box when you have played each piece, so that you keep trying new ones.

Things to check before starting a piece of sight reading:
- The time signature – are you going to count in twos, threes or fours?
- The tempo – how fast should you count? Remember to count yourself in for two whole bars.
- The key signature – are there any black notes to remember?
- Are there any accidentals, and do any of them affect later notes in the same bar?
- The fingering given for the start of the piece – use this to get both hands into position.
- The dynamics – where should you play loudly and where softly?
- Any legato, staccato and accent markings.
- Are there any patterns in the music that will make it easier to read, and are there any leaps or rests that may be tricky?

Things to help you practise:
- Try playing slowly at first if that helps, and build up to a faster speed later:
  a regular pulse is more important than the speed at which you play.
- Try getting the notes and rhythm right first, and then play it again adding in changes of dynamics and details such as legato, staccato and accents.
- Try not to look at your fingers as you play, but keep your eyes fixed on the music.
  Get used to feeling your way around the keyboard without looking at it.
  Look ahead in the music to spot what is coming up.

Things to remember in the exam:
- The examiner will give you half a minute to look at the piece before starting to play.
  Use this time to try out the music – don't be afraid to do this, the examiner won't be listening!
  Play the opening and the ending, and perhaps any tricky bars.
- The examiner will tell you when to finish the try out and start playing for real.
- If you keep to a regular pulse at the marked speed and get most of the notes right,
  you will pass your sight reading!
- You will be heading for a top mark for sight reading if you *also* include clear contrasts in the dynamics, and any differences between staccato and legato.
- Keep concentrating until you have given the last note its full length.
- **Try not to hesitate, even if you make a mistake.**
  Hesitations and stops are the most common reasons for a disappointing mark in sight reading.

Good luck with your Grade 2 sight reading!